Harlequin Rabbits as Pets

The Handy Guide for Harlequin Rabbits

General Info, Purchasing, Care, Marketing, Keeping, Health, Supplies, Food, Breeding and More Included!

By Lolly Brown

Copyrights and Trademarks

Disclaimer and Legal Notice

Foreword

Welcome to wonderful and colorful world of harlequin rabbits. We trust that you are here in the hopes of finding out more about these fuzzy, furry creatures, the harlequin because we aim to let you in on anything and everything you need to know about these lovable rabbits with the funky colors.

Initially shown in France back in the late 1800's, the harlequin has come a long way since then. It was later introduced to the United States of America in the early 1900's and has continued to capture many a-hearts all over the world. It continues to fascinate many rabbit lovers and families alike who have chosen to raise these lovable bunnies for pets.

Come with us on a journey of getting to know these adorable fur-balls and discover what it takes to raise them. Learn about everything it would need to live a happy life with you and your family and get into the mindset of raising a couple of them with confidence and eager openness. Let's dig in deeper, shall we?

Table of Contents

Chapter One: Understanding Harlequin Rabbits

Discovered and ultimately introduced to society in France as far back as the 1880's, the harlequin is lauded to be one of the oldest domesticated rabbits amongst all these furry hoppers. Harlequin rabbits are the oldest rabbits around. They have a commercial type physique and are uniquely marked with colors of orange and black or lilac, chocolate or blue. Others are white and lilac, blue, chocolate or black. They are intelligent rabbits suitable for first time pet owners, are good with children and perfect for apartment dwellers. Having had lived side by side or in very close proximity to humans, harlequins have captured many a hearts from then up to the present day. It will become clearer why it is so, as you read on and find out.

Facts about Harlequin Rabbits

This colorful rabbit breed is acknowledged by both the British Rabbit Council as well as the American Rabbit Breeder's Association. It was originally called the Japanese rabbit but that name was quickly replaced when the 2nd world war began, to deviate its association from warring countries.

Often referred to as the "clown" or the "jester" of rabbits, you will have to wonder "what sort of amusing tricks do they do to have earned them such a moniker?" Well, it is not so much named for its antics as it is for its appearance. As mentioned earlier, the harlequin is known for being one of the most colorful of rabbits.

The harlequin ideally would have two colors dividing its face giving it a different profile on one side of its face to the other - hence the jester-like appearance. Its body sports what seems like almost tiger-like markings of stripes or strikes in the various colors each individual rabbit is born with, which we shall delve into more in a little while.

General Body Types of Rabbits

You would think that a rabbit is a rabbit is a rabbit but there are different types of rabbits and each sort have their own unique look, colors, shapes and body types. They may share some general traits and overall characteristics but physically, they are quite different in physique. There are five classified body types of a rabbit.

The harlequin is what experts would call the commercial body type which is chunky, robust and stocky. It has a wide head with upturned ears that ideally should alternate whatever colors the rabbit sports. The harlequin is a medium to large sized rabbit and would ideally weigh anywhere between six to nine pounds. Other examples of rabbits with a commercial body type would be the French Lop, the Palomino, the Satin, the Californian, and others.

Another rabbit body type would be the compact body. This rabbit body type is roundish-looking with shoulders that are hardly visible. Categorized under this body type are the English Angora, the America Fuzzy Lop, the Dwarf Hotot, the Netherland Dwarf, the Silver, and others.

Falling under the cylindrical body type, which displays a straight-line body, having no rise and does not taper from its profile, would be the Colored Vienna, The White Vienna and the Himalayan rabbit. It is interesting to know that only one rabbit representative is acknowledged by the ARBA while the BRC recognizes two.

The body type which shows itself to look like giants, as compared to the others mentioned in this section, is the Mandolin (as referred to by the British Rabbit Council) or the Semi-Arch. Some examples of these rabbits which have a distract arch just beyond its shoulders would be the Beveren, the English Lop, the Giant Chinchilla, the Golden Glavot and others.

And last, but not the least would be the full-arch body type. These rabbits, like the Britannia Petite, the English Spot, the Checkered Giant, the Tan and others sport a fully arched back and is built for speed and agility. Let's read up more about our focus for this book, and check out the types of harlequin rabbits.

Types of Harlequin Rabbits

As with other rabbit species which typically come in more than one sort, so does the harlequin. There are two of them and each has their own name which makes them distinct from each other.

The Magpie harlequin rabbit is the sort that has a base color of white and is mixed in with either a chocolate, blue, black or lilac color. Whereas the Japanese is the other sort of harlequin rabbit which is typically orange based in color mixed in with a lilac, chocolate, blue or black color. These individual coloration markings are seen as bars or bands on their bodies and sometimes it is a combination of both bars and bands giving them that tiger-like appearance.

History

The docile harlequin like all rabbits find its originations out in the wild. But these rabbits have served quite a purpose alongside humans since its discovery. It presently continues to capture the attention of rabbit-lovers all over who keep these multi colored rabbits as pets. The harlequin was developed to be the rabbit we know it today in France during the late 1800's and was put under the limelight in the 1880's. The harlequin came about when Dutch rabbits of the tortoiseshell colored sort were bred with rabbits of the wild. It is considered to be one of the pioneering rabbit breeds. It is also a rabbit breed that makes for good fosters since they are open to welcoming into their brood a rabbit that isn't necessarily theirs.

Sometime during the war time era, because meat was scarce, rationed and difficult to obtain, harlequins were sought out for their meat. A chilling thought for anyone who owns a couple of these rabbits presently. But that has been a while back and now harlequins are bred largely to be kept and raised as pets.

Chapter Two: Keeping Harlequin Rabbits

Owning a Harlequin Rabbit can bring so much joy to each member of the family with many hours of fun and years of learning. Living with one, or highly recommended - two, harlequins as pets is fine in most countries and US states. The game changes drastically if you intend to breed the rabbits and what your purposes are. Let's look into details of these laws a little deeper.

License Requirements

Understanding legalities, regulations and rights is important when keeping pets. Many pets commonly available in the pet trade are bought and sold with restrictions or licenses and this is true for rabbits as well. In this chapter, we shall be discussing the regulations and restrictions for buying, selling, keeping, and raising rabbits both in the United States and the United Kingdom.

United States Licensing for Rabbits

The Animal Welfare Act takes into effect when a breeder purveys rabbits costing more than $500 a year. Therefore if you have been breeding and selling rabbits costing roughly that amount of over, you will need to get a license; getting a license means that you will have to comply with housing and animal care regulations as well as restrictions and laws.

Alabama

Giving away or selling young rabbits in Alabama for pet purposes can land a person a misdemeanor violation which will be meted out with punishment according to Alabama laws. It is also illegal to give rabbits away as prize.

So if you find yourself at a state fair and you are given a rabbit as a prize, you might want to look into that.

Arkansas

In Arkansas, it is illegal to for anyone to give away baby rabbits under two months of age to anyone. It is also illegal for anyone to dye a rabbit and pass this off as their natural color. Breeders who have satisfied the requirements of state laws on breeding requirements are exempt from this law (except for the dying of color). A class C misdemeanor is imposed upon a guilty verdict if an individual is found to be guilty of breaking this law.

Arizona

The Arizona State Legislature deems it illegal to sell any animal on public causeways, property close to an expressway, by the highway or at a park. If selling from a privately owned establishment or property, the individual making the sale has to have outright consent and agreement from the owner or the renter of the establishment, whether indoors or outdoors. This does not apply to livestock gatherings, auctions, fairs or rodeos. A person who is found to have broken this law will have to pay a penalty of about $50. The city of Phoenix deems it illegal to sell trade, or gift rabbits below two months of age. It is also unlawful to change the rabbits color to suit it for barter, sale or to offer as a gift. Transporting of rabbits into the city is also prohibited. Licensed breeders who have complied with the sanitation codes of the city of Phoenix and follow the Board of Health laws are not affected by these controls.

It is unlawful to change hands, purvey, purchase and transfer to another owner any animal in any public place in Santa Cruz County, Arizona. This mandate does not apply to 4H events, shows and exhibits for animals, county fairs and other occasions that fall under and are manned by the Arizona Revised Statues. Individuals who are guilty of going against these commands shall be guilty of a class 2 violation.

These same rules apply in Nogales, Arizona, as stated by the Nogales Code of statutes. The penalties for breaking should anyone are found to break these ordinances will be fined. No business is allowed to give permission to any individual to give away or purvey a rabbit at any business establishment inside the borders of the city of Sedona nor is it allowed for any individual or business to offer an animal as price to entice foot traffic to their place of business.

The Humane Society of Sedona as well as its moving pet assumption is exempt from this condition.

California

Unless an individual or establishment is allowed by the state of California to barter, purvey or give away an animal, no one is allowed to hand over, exchange, or sell rabbits on any premises. Coloring an animal to alter its appearance for purposes of gaining profit, to gift or trade in any establishment is unlawful as well as stated by the California Codes.

No individual or business establishment in Healsburg, California is given permission to trade, purvey or gift any animals unless they have obtained proper licenses that gives them the right to do so. Individuals in Lathrope, California is not permitted to prize out, sell, display or trade any animal or to entice other individuals to join contests, enter business establishments or attract clientele.

It is not permissible in Lathrope to gift young rabbits as a promotion unless the individual offering the promotion has a visibly, readable note that states the rabbit, altered by dying or otherwise, can be returned after 30 days without any charges. The county of LA, California does not allow any individual who temporarily rents a stall at a swap meet to exhibit or advocate the sale of rabbits. It is also deemed unlawful for anyone from an animal shelter to purvey, take in or trade animals without the consent of the establishment director.

Rabbits under two months of age are not prohibited to be handed out as gift, to be sold or traded nor is it permitted to alter the rabbit's innate coloration. Brining rabbits into the Los Angeles County is also not allowed. Only LA establishments properly outfitted to trade, sell and are run by accredited breeders in the county of Los Angeles are allowed to purvey, deal or give out rabbits as well as exhibit them with the intent of promoting better animal production and trade.

The city-county of San Francisco Anyone found guilty of going against provisions with regard to displaying, trading, purveying, gifting rabbits, whether color-modified or not, shall be breaking the ordinance of the city-county, guilty of a misdemeanor and will be fined up to $50.

Colorado

Colorado Statutes read that unless an individual is given permission to do so, no one is to take in, exchange or purchase rabbits under 4-week old. No one in Fort Collins is to lure or motive anyone to participating in a contest, or promote an establishment for profit, or make business deal exchanges using a rabbit unless they are duly licensed establishments under ordinance. The same rules apply in Lafayette. This law refers back to state laws against cruelty to animals. No one is to have, purvey, gift or exhibit any rabbit which has been color-modified to homes looking for pets or individuals looking to gift said animal.

Connecticut

Anyone caught passing off a dyed rabbit as its natural color whether as gift or for purchase intended to be brought out of state or country will be penalized and will have to pay $150 as stated by this state's General Statutes.

Delaware

No person in Wilmington is given permission to hand out any rabbits nor is it allowed to use rabbits for promotional purposes, to purvey or entice clientele for the purpose of making profit. It is also against the law to give away, offer up, trade less than half a dozen rabbits that are below 2 months of age. Another ordinance states that no dyed rabbit is to be given away, sold or traded. These laws are not applied to commercial breeding facilities with the appropriate license to operate.

District of Columbia

Regulations in the District of Columbia read that no one is to purvey any young rabbit whether of natural color or dyed to appear a different shade. No rabbits under 3 months and two weeks are to be sold unless it is used for scientific research and this same rule applies to purveyors of rabbits under 16 weeks unless used for agricultural advancement.

Florida

The state of Florida does not allow any person to synthetically alter the coloration of a rabbit at any stage of its life. Nor is anyone allowed to bring into the state a color-altered rabbit, no matter what age it is. It is also not permissible to sell or give away rabbits that are under 2 months of age. These conditions are not applicable to rabbits which are used neither for health preservation reasons nor for agricultural reasons given that these entities are duly equipped with correct housing and facilities. Any person in violation is guilty of a second degree misdemeanor and will be meted the equal punishment according to the law. Miami further restricts the ownership, purvey and exchange of rabbit that have been synthetically colored.

Georgia

Only licensed animal and pet societies as well as animal owners are allowed to purvey and put up for purchase in any temporary public, as flea markets, fairs or private establishments, as animal rescue centers and shelters as well as retail stores.

Anyone intending to show animals as in petting zoos and animal shows will need to obtain proper licensure and be agreeable to spot inspections. They are to follow all the rules as stated by the guidelines to exhibit and not put on display any animals which are ill. These licensed individuals will need to have the services of a vet on hand should an animal show to be ill. Residents, transients and visitors in Athens -Clarke County is not permitted to use an animal to invoke public traffic with intent to make profit. No one is allowed to use an animal as prize to entice participation in any sort of contest.

In Cobb County, Georgia only licensed recue centers, vets, dealers of pets, humane groups who have been duly registered and have been given permission to do so can hand out or sell animals in public or private establishments. So goes these restrictions in Jackson County, Georgia. In addition only those who have been able to get licenses are permitted to show animals intended for exhibitions in circuses, petting zoos and animal shows. Controls are taken that all measures of health and safety have been satisfied and animals are not harmed. Giving away animals as a prize is forbidden in Spalding County, Georgia.

Illinois

It is against the law to purvey, offer and hand out artificially colored rabbits or give them away as prize for winning a competition. Anyone found to break these ordinances will be found guilty of a class B misdemeanor. Any violations after the first are meted with a harsher penalty.

Only licensed pet retailers, breeders, societies and animal facilities may exhibit and purvey for retail rabbits under conditions that the rabbit has undergone proper medical inspection and has been given the correct inoculation along with the dates these vaccination were given, that the rabbit's medical records state its age, sex, breed. That the place of the rabbit's birth rescues or impounded is stated.

These details are to be explicitly stated on paper by the pet retailer and hand over a copy to the interested purchasing individual, whilst keeping the original copy for a length of two years and is on hand when city officials come around for inspection. Any retailer selling rabbits is to post all the details in relation to the rabbit where it can be seen and read as stipulated by law.

Individuals in the St. Charles are not permitted to purvey, offer, and hand out artificially colored rabbits. It is also unlawful for anyone to give a rabbit away as prize to a winner of a neither competition nor are rabbits to be used to induce attraction to an establishment that aims to profit. So goes for Kane County with an additional penalty to anyone receiving such a rabbit and keeps it.

It is not permitted for anyone to artificially color and pass off a rabbit for sale or give away in McHenry County. Nor should anyone give a rabbit away as prize for winning, use a rabbit to entice trade without registration 48 hours before any event.

Indiana

The Indiana Code prohibits color alteration and the transportation of rabbits under 8 weeks of age. Anyone breaking this rule will be guilty of a class b misdemeanor. This does not apply to retailers and breeders with proper facilities fitted to care for juvenile rabbits.

New Mexico

Selling rabbits in pet shops is prohibited with exceptions during the months of March and April. The codes across the states are closely alike with minor differences from one to another. It is best to check out the regulations and ordinances of your state with regard to purchasing, raising, transporting, importing, exporting and living with rabbits as pets. It is strongly advised that any person or group of people intending to breed and raise rabbits get in touch with their local authorities to find out about the restrictions, guidelines and ordinances of their home state regarding purchase, selling, raising, transporting and giving away of rabbits. Breaking these rules, ordinances or guidelines will constitute penalties, misdemeanor to criminal acts and will be judged and fined according to the state's laws.

United Kingdom Licensing for Rabbits

The Department for Environment Food and Rural Affairs has a set of guidelines which state that any persons caring for rabbits must have adequate facilities to safely house and rear rabbits. These facilities are to be outfitted with non-toxic materials which may cause illness or poison the rabbits. Site inspectors may call in for a visit by making an appointment with handlers and breeders but may also show up unannounced should a complaint be lodged against a particular rabbit facility.

Guidelines go on to state that no rabbit under 4 weeks should be disturbed that any unsafe foods should be reported and disposed of properly. In the event of a rabbit expiring on site, there are guidelines to follow on how to dispose of it. A veterinarian must be on hand to care for any ailing rabbits or at the very least there must be a competent staff on hand who will be able to do the job until a vet is able to get to the site to pay mind and give medical attention to the sick rabbit.

Rabbits who are housed are to be inspected regularly and not allow any rabbit showing signs of illness to be left alone and unattended. Rabbits are to be protected from other animals, providing them with spacious suitable enclosures which keep rodents and predators out. The rabbits are to be inspected thoroughly for ear mites and ears should be free of encrustations and dirt.

The administration of vaccinations is only to be carried out by competent individuals and have to be mindful about not causing any injury to the rabbit whilst administering vaccinations. It is strongly advised that rabbit tags be done with ink instead of bands which later get tight as the rabbit neither grows nor is it suggested to use ear rings as these cause distress and unnecessary pain to the bunny.

Tooth and nail trimming is to be carried out by trained and competent individual, or ideally a vet. Handling rabbits should be gentle and humane at all times paying mind that handlers not be rough or brusque when lifting or carrying the animal. Housing should have adequate space allowing for free movement when the rabbit eats and enclosures should be high enough for the rabbit to sit comfortably with its ears not touching the roof of the cage. Rabbits should be protected from the elements and enclosures must be correctly outfitted with necessary heaters, vents, lighting and temperature controlled monitors.

Enclosures are to be regularly cleaned out of soiled bedding and disinfected. It should be free from any mars, like splinters or wires that stick out which could cause injury to the rabbits. Outdoor enclosures should also be outfitted to protect the rabbits from the elements, free from drafts and that rabbits have dry, clean bedding all the time. If using a wire mesh floor, there are measurement specs to be adhered to and followed. All equipment like heaters, vents, temperature regulator are to be inspected routinely, and should any of these fail, it should be immediately replaced. Wires are to be kept away from the rabbit's reach to, ideally beneath the ground where the rabbits will not be able to reach them.

Before restocking, facility operators are to clean and disinfect all enclosures, making sure to reduce any sort of infection and contagion from spreading to the next batch of rabbits. All facilities staff is to be trained to handle emergencies and should know what to do in case of one.

How Many Harlequin Rabbits Should You Keep?

If you are the kind of person whose lifestyle has you living most of your time indoors and seldom leave your home for long stretches of time then the harlequin is a good choice rabbit for you. However, you will probably be busy with other things that you would need to take care of throughout the day as well. So let's find out how many of these rabbits you can raise.

Harlequin rabbits can get pretty lonely by its lonesome and would fare quite well if it was paired with another of its kind. Not only would they be a source of joy to look at for you, they would also gladly keep the company of another and possibly start a family!

Like most rabbits they are pretty high maintenance and would take a decent chunk of your time, and a portion of your finances, as you tend and care for them and their needs. So you will want to consider the time you can spend each day cleaning out cages, feeding and grooming them. Balance your monthly budget as well because taking in any pet to raise has its cost.

Do Harlequin Rabbits Get Along with Other Pets?

These rabbits are better off paired with another to keep each other company and engaged when not enjoying some time alone or the pleasure of your company. As for getting along with other pets, this goes both ways; add to your research and consideration any existing pets you may have and find out if they are rabbit friends or rabbit aggressors.

There are some canines and felines which have an innate instinct of going after rabbits and that would be a disaster if it happened in your home! However, there have been many reports of dog or cat owners who have taken in a rabbit and have had no issues. It all boils down to knowing the individual behaviors and personalities of your pets, as well as supervision and observation on your end.

If you are truly set on integrating a harlequin rabbit to your home with established pets, you will have to take the time, and have a good measure of patience to help them integrate peacefully, get to know each other and live harmoniously. The rule of thumb is to always be present when all pets are in one space and to never leave them alone by themselves at any cost.

Costs of Keeping a Harlequin

Like most rabbit sorts, harlequins will take up a considerable amount of time to maintain, feed, and groom. Aside from those things, you will need to spend a considerable amount of time with them to train and socialize them. It will take quite a bit of sacrifice on your end to pen them and their needs into your once usual routine and you will have to switch your schedule around a bit.

They will need to have the attention of a vet periodically to check their health and wellness. They are not expensive, but they and their daily needs will amount to a sizable chunk of your finances. But taking them in and raising them will have their own precious, priceless rewards.

Initial Costs

You want to be able to sort out your finances and get this straight before committing to raising any sort of pet. A rabbit is not exactly what you would call low maintenance both in terms or care and health.

You would initially have to think about buying all sundries and supplies your rabbits would need to welcome it to a home that is ready, willing and wanting its company. A harlequin rabbit costs anywhere from $30-$50 and the price may be higher for a show breed sort, as much as $75-$100.

A hutch, unless you are making it yourself could put you out anywhere between $50-$100. Think about looking for hutch ideas online because many harlequin owners have done the same and has saved them a pretty penny whilst allowing them to fashion intricate hutches that blend in with their indoor or outdoor furniture.

Vet costs and inoculation expenses would also be an initial financial factor you would have to be ready for. Rabbit vaccine against RVHD is recommended to be given twice a year, or every 6 to 12 months. You would also need an indoor cage to keep your harlequin on days and seasons when it is too cold for it to play and foray in an outdoor hutch. A cage could cost anywhere from $25-$45 dollars. It is never recommended to purchase a second hand cage or hutch lest the rabbit that previously used it had contracted illness.

Feeding dishes and drip bottles for water are other sundries apart from a sturdy brush and a pair of nail clippers which you would need to take care of your harlequin rabbit's grooming needs. You will also want to invest on your pet's own blanket or towel to use when you need to wash up and wipe down your harlequin.

You will want to invest on a tiny shed to place inside its cage and hutch where it can scoot and hide in when it feels vulnerable or when it is tired and needs a rest. Litter boxes, and a few of them might we add, are essential sundries that you would need to invest on because you don't want your rabbit to randomly poop inside it hutch or cage and most especially when it is allowed to roam any of the rooms you would have rabbit-proofed.

Lastly you want to be ready with a bowl of pellets and food for when you are ready to take home your harlequin. Another purchase to add to its food list would be treats which will come in handy when you begin training your harlequin, as you will read later on in this book.

Monthly Costs

The amount of money you will be spending on a monthly basis to maintain, raise and keep your harlequin goes down considerably on a month to month basis.

However, we advise that you set aside a portion of your finances which you can dip into later for booster shots, vet visits and other sundries you may find your harlequin may need.

Toys will definitely be another expense you want to put money aside for as you will soon discover that your harlequin may not exactly take to liking the ones that it has been provided with initially. Experiment with stuff you find around the house, but make sure that these are made of non-toxic materials because you certainly don't want a sick rabbit on your hands and an unexpected rush visit to the vet if it does get ill from any chemical substances stemming from the use of unchecked toys you give it.

Food would be a cost to add to your monthly bills because once you figure out the sorts of pellet preference of your rabbit, you will want to stock up on these along with fresh veggies, treats and fruits that it is allowed and should have. Vitamins and supplements would also be something you will have to acquire after given recommendations by your vet.

Pros and Cons of Harlequin Rabbits

The downside of owning harlequin rabbits would be that you would need to take the time to clean out its cage on a daily basis to avoid germs from propagating in it. It is also not as easy to potty or litter train a rabbit so you might be scooping out poop and soiled bedding more often than if you had a cat. Another con is that, without proper handling, socialization and training a rabbit can get pretty aggressive, so make sure that you take the time at the beginning of the integration to teach it social manners and allow it to get used to the presence of other people of the family.

The upside to having a harlequin rabbit join your ranks is that with proper socialization, it can be the friendliest, most amiable, docile, intelligent creature you would know. With time and patience, you WILL be able to litter train it, it can learn to understand its name when it is called out, and is a wonderful pet for first timers. It is also a great pet to have around children as long as the children are made to understand that all pets, as with people, need to be treated with respect and kindness.

Chapter Two: Keeping Harlequin Rabbits

Chapter Three: Purchasing Harlequin Rabbits

You wouldn't be reading this book this far if you weren't really into getting a harlequin integrated in your life. Seeing a harlequin and knowing how easy-going it is, it is no wonder you are considering it. Determining early on what your intent is in raising a harlequin rabbit will be a pretty important decision to make as well, especially if you have intentions of showing off your rabbit at shows. On the other hand if you are looking to raise one, we advise that you consider getting two because harlequins thrive so much better in pairs. Not only do they get to keep the company of another rabbit like it, you also get double the fun.

Knowing who you should be talking to, where to get these uniquely different harlequins as well as what you should be looking out for during this time of your search are important details you want to know and learn because a lot hinges on talking to the right person at the onset of your quest. Doing so, dealing with an honest, humane breeder that is, coupled with optimum care from your end will ensure a healthy, long living bunny.

Where Can You Buy Harlequin Rabbits?

You can buy from pet shops, flea markets, backyard rabbit breeders or private breeders, rabbit rescue centers, and from dedicated rabbit hobbyists. The most popular place to buy Harlequin rabbits or any animal is of course from your local pet shops. However, most breeders do not recommend and in fact highly discourage people to purchase rabbits from these pet shops simply because the store owners don't know anything about particular rabbit breeds, and more often than not the animals sold in pet shops are not being properly taken care of. They're probably selling or breeding rabbits for the sole purpose of making money off of it, and not really taking the time to care for the rabbit's particular needs. Many people have had bad experiences purchasing pets from these local shops because most of the time rabbits die after they were brought home from the pet stores due to lack of adequate care. Pet stores also tend to take away the bunnies sometimes too early from their mother which is why they may be prone to many illnesses or has an unhealthy condition. Perhaps the only advantage of buying from pet stores is that it's near your house and you can get supplies any time with less hassle but as much as possible do not buy from pet shops.

Another popular place to purchase a Harlequin is from flea markets. Again these are not highly recommended because normally rabbits being sold in flea markets are of mixed rabbit breeds. So if you want a Harlequin breed but you are not that familiar with it, chances are you'll end up buying another kind of rabbit breed.

Another major disadvantage is that you don't know where these rabbits came from, you don't know their previous living condition, if they're healthy or not, and the breeder may not have taken care these rabbits properly. Yes, you can buy cheap rabbit breeds in flea markets that probably come in all shapes and sizes but it's highly discouraged. If you want to buy a Harlequin that could possibly be cheaper and you can also be assured of its quality, then go get them from rabbit rescue centers. This is a good place if you want to adopt a rabbit, perhaps the main advantage is that you can actually save a life if you decided to adopt a bunny.

When it comes to quality, you can be assured that these bunnies are well taken care of, and you'll get to know the rabbit's health history since they are being kept by professionals. Sometimes rabbits from rescue centers are already spayed or neutered so you won't have a problem with that anymore. But it may not be a good idea to adopt a rabbit from a shelter if you want to breed rabbits or join a show.

One of the common and better places to purchase a rabbit is from backyard rabbit breeders. The reason for this is because these breeders are small time rabbit keepers, which means that they usually have only a couple of litter that is being sold. It also means that since they only take care of a couple of litters, you can be assured of its quality and health.

You can also go back and ask the breeders questions in terms of the previous living condition, the food, the age, the breed, the health status etc. Be careful though because there are still some backyard breeders who only breeds rabbits because they want to get rid of their excess litter or just sell them. You can also buy from rabbit enthusiasts because these people are generally the go – to place of any keepers who already have had some experience when it comes to buying rabbits. Dedicated hobbyists usually have larger places and they seriously know a lot about a particular breed that they're selling. These are the people who are reputable breeders because they don't just sell their pets to anyone; they also like to make sure that their bunnies will go to good homes.

They care for their pets so much that they'll go the extra mile of making sure that you'll be ready to raise the bunnies that they bred. The only disadvantage is that the rabbits can be quite expensive, but you can be guaranteed of the quality, the health, and also the support system if you have further inquiries about the rabbit breed you purchase. It is worth investing in though because you won't have to worry about the health and   wellness of your pet in the long run and also save you a lot of money.

Choosing a Reputable Harlequin Rabbit Breeder

Breeders of upstanding repute will adhere to rules for releasing harlequins with assurance and guarantees that you are getting a healthy bunny to bring home. Not dealing with a reputable, recently successful breeder will most likely because unnecessary vet visits which equates to a pile up of medical bills.

Be aware of questions you want to ask your breeder, like what sort of foods it had been fed, when the rabbit was weaned, what their methods are for breeding rabbits and if initial inoculation against RVHD and myxomatosis. A good breeder will be ready to answer these questions with confidence and any breeder who gives flowery or unsure answers should be shunned from your list.

Upstanding breeders will also have their own set of questions to ask you. "Why" you ask? Well, that is because these breeders, as much as they are making a little money out of the purchase are also concerned about the homes the rabbits will be joining. They are set on improving the breed and mindful that the rabbits are not just a whim purchase that will be left alone in a cage unattended by unmindful buyers.

Breeders thoughtful of the rabbits would have done the necessary initial procedures such as providing initial vet care, inoculation and would have provided the rabbit's conducive housing. They would not feel iffy about allowing a request to visit their facilities and would even welcome it. They would have sanitary facilities, adequate and correct lodgings and area to breed, raise and care for their rabbits and would have the appropriate licenses needed by most breeders. They would be compliant with laws and regulations of their state regarding breeding methods, and have the proper facilities for this purpose. And they will never release a rabbit under 12 weeks old to anyone.

On the other hand fly by night breeders would ask you about how you intend to handle payments and would give you shady answers to the questions which are important to answer. They would be unsure about many things and this would show in their hesitance to answer you directly. Any breeder who is more concerned about your credit card payment going through is a breeder worth running away from.

Another red flag of unscrupulous breeders is that they would be unwilling to allow you to visit their facilities, opting instead to do business online. If a breeder refuses you a scheduled access to their site, take it as a sign that you should look for someone else.

Breeders who are just in it for the money would not be able to give you any sort of guarantee should anything go wrong later. They just want the rabbit out of their hands and money in their pocket. Be aware of these red flags and you would almost certainly be getting a healthy well socialized rabbit to bring home.

You should also make sure that the place or facility should be clean and well organized which means that the rabbits should have hutches of their own to reside in and to avoid being crowded. If you are talking to someone who owns a huge rabbitry, the owner should always keep everything on track, and has rabbitry records for all the bunnies. Rabbitry management chores should be done in a time efficient manner so that everything is in place. Most importantly the owners should have a fun and enjoyable rabbit raising experience.

Selecting a Healthy Harlequin Rabbit

Spotting a healthy harlequin is essential at this point because this would mean better chances of your harlequins enjoying a good life of sound health. Knowing what to look for and what to look out for are things we will be discussing here so get ready to come closer to making a confident decision about taking home a pair to raise yourself.

First off you want to select a rabbit that is old enough and has been properly weaned in a timely fashion. Old enough means that it should be at least 8 weeks old, since this is an acceptable age for it to be weaned off its mother. Any younger and a rabbit could show stress which may result to an ill rabbit. You also want to buy from a breeder who has separated the males from the females and not just randomly picked up from a litter of many. The risk of bringing home a pregnant rabbit could be costly to you as much as it would be a surprise. You need to be ready to know how to care for a pregnant rabbit and know what to expect and do, otherwise this could spell disaster.

You want to check that all the rabbits in the cage are active and healthy because if there is one looking sickly then chances are it has contaminated the rest and would eventually get sick as well. A lethargic bunny could be sick and whatever it has could've already been passed on to the rest.

Healthy rabbits are alert and mobile and would be aware and react accordingly to a new presence in its midst. It would show itself active and mobile, curious yet rightfully skittish when new people are around. Both its nose and eyes are to be spotless with no signs of discharge. It should not be sneezing or sniffling.

Check its vent because fecal matter matted to its skin and fur signals a rabbit could be suffering from diarrhea. Both its front teeth should line up straight and not be crooked and the upper front teeth or incisors should overlap with the lower front teeth. Rabbit dropping should be firm and dry and not runny. There shouldn't be any bald spots anywhere on its body, no scarring or nicks on its ears or anywhere else for that matter. Its ears should also be clean and free of any form of dirt or wax.

Do not rush into buying a rabbit instead take your time to inspect and check out the rabbit for any telltale signs that it may be ill.

Chapter Four: Caring for Your Harlequin Rabbits

The harlequin rabbit is a curious learner and seeker of all things new and old. It will not only inspect a space once, but repeatedly do so when given the chance to roam free. So make sure that you rabbit proof the spaces it will be allowed to explore. Rabbit proofing your home means removing any chemicals or cleaning solutions your rabbit may come across and ingest, inhale or come in contact with its skin. Make sure that wires are covered with hard plastic tubing or repositioned higher up, on the ceiling preferably, and out of your rabbits inquisitive reach.

Make sure that there are no splintered woods, toxic plastic, noxious paint chips that it may gnaw on which would cause it to inure itself or get sick from since your rabbit will be doing a lot of that. To avoid this from happening, make sure that you provide it with safe tree branches and twigs which it can chew on and would help trim down its never ending teeth growth.

Check your home for any open vents that the rabbit could enter and get lost in and be sure that you cover them. Check your door and window screens for any broken wires that are sticking out which may snag your rabbit and cause injury to it. Make sure that there are no holes or gaps it can wriggle into or escape out of.

Habitat Requirements for Harlequin Rabbits

Harlequins, like most domesticated pets of today originate from the wild and would need to somehow be allowed to roam "free", under your watchful eye. It needs to be let out once in a while to feel the cool of grass and earth on its little bunny paws. But it also needs a place to retreat to when all tired out from a day of romping and playing. Your home, or at least part of it, will also be partly occupied by your harlequin so make sure that you outfit spaces it is allowed to roam and that these areas of your home is rabbit proofed for its safety and yours. Make sure you have enough litter boxes and locate them in areas where each one is accessible to your rabbits as well because, seriously. Who wants to step on poop and scatter that all over the place? So limit spaces if you don't want a larger place to clean up.

What sort of space does it need? Should you keep it cooped up all times of the day or allow it to rule over the household? What will it take for you to set up, outfit and provide your harlequins with comfortable digs? Those are answers you will find in these next sections of this chapter.

Ideal Rabbit Cage

A cage that is keeps it safe from accidental escape and one that allows it enough leg room to move around is what your harlequins will need. Depending on the size of the harlequins you keep will determine the size of its cage. Aside from these essential housing needs, "ideal" also means optimum in every manner - therefore, cage maintenance and sanitation is very important. Make sure that there are no mosquitoes or flies infesting your harlequin's cage. Flies can burrow under the rabbits skin and lay larvae causing it skin infections and worse, whereas mosquitoes are carriers of hemorrhagic fever which is deadly to your rabbit.

That being said and getting back to cage size, you will want to think ahead and anticipate the growth rate of your rabbit and factor that future size-to-be when you build your rabbit cage. Ideally a 30x24x15 cage would suffice, but it never hurts to get or build a bigger one. A dream cage would not only have the space your harlequins would need for a good stretch it should also have a shady nook where it can curl up in when it needs to rest. Make sure that use soft bedding that would cushion its feet. Avoid wire mesh based cages as this material will hurt and may injure your rabbits.

Make sure that the cage material is sturdy enough and outfitted with all the necessary fittings to keep it occupied so that it doesn't pick on the wires.

Indoor Cages vs. Outdoor Hutches

Your harlequin is going to need comfortable, spacious cages and hutches that would allow it to do all the fun stuff it needs to in order for it to thrive well and satisfy its exercise and amusement needs. You will want to make sure that you provide them with the proper kind of digs that would allow them to be themselves.

Indoor cages should be of considerable size that your harlequin is able to move around with ease. It should be spacious enough that it can take rests comfortably and have a space where it can eat in peace. Make sure that the cages of your harlequins are kept clean because healthy rabbits have become sick from unmaintained, unsanitary, unkempt and smelly cages. A soiled cage left for too long is a breeding ground for all sorts of bacteria and fungi that will get into your harlequins system.

So goes for outdoor hutches. If you have a big space of land, you may want to consider going the extra mile and build an outdoor hatch for your rabbits. Make sure that the hatch has an elevated part off the ground where they can exercise their little legs with a ramp or a cat-walk where they can clamber down from and feel grass and earth beneath their feet.

If you live in a limited space, like a flat, fret not. Take stock of the space you can allot where your rabbits can roam free while you are at home. At the very least you can use a low fence that would border the area and give them a good amount of play space. Lay it with soft bedding, set out their food and drinking dishes, and go about doing your own thing with one eye and ear closely trained and attuned to them, especially if you have other established pets in the family. Other rabbit owners have come up with ingenious ideas of incorporating their rabbit cages and hutches into their home design. An old, low bookshelf refurbished and fitted with safety boarders and wire, an old television case, an old fashioned hi-fi housing - the possibilities are endless!

Recommended Cage Accessories

Like other pets, rabbits will need sundries which it will be using for a long time so be wise about your choices from the onset to avoid a pile up of purchases that go to waste. Admittedly you may have to experiment with some purchases at the beginning, but this is where we come in to give you the low down on what will minimize the cost and cut the time you need to set up a suitable habitat for your rabbits.

Some inexpensive sundries you have to provide for your harlequins are chew toys or face the fact of your furniture, carpet and electrical wires being chewed by your rabbits. You want to give it pieces of apple, aspen or willow branches to chew on. Toilet paper tubing is also some materials which you can easily find around the house and regularly replace with almost no cost to you.

Make sure that you have long lasting, non-wearing, wide-based ceramic feeding dishes and dripper drinking bottles with fresh and clean water. The ceramic dish is a good choice since it lasts long and is less likely to topple over when your rabbit eats out of it. A dripper bottle gives the convenience of allowing more space in the cage and easier access to your rabbit when it needs a drink.

Make a space where they can dig and burrow and allow for them to do what is natural to them. Outfit your rabbit cages with nooks and hideaways where they can retreat to when they feel frightened or need a good recharging rest. You also want to line your rabbit cages with hay as and chewing twigs and stumps because these help file down the teeth of your harlequins. Without tools to help your harlequin file down its teeth naturally, its teeth may get too large for its mouth causing it to injure itself when it bites down or prevent the harlequin from closing its mouth properly.

Chapter Five: Feeding Your Harlequin Rabbit

Feeding your harlequin the proper foods to help it grow healthy is essential knowledge you need to know so that you are in a position to provide it with the balanced and correct nourishment it needs. The proper feeding portions are also very important to understand because underfeeding and overfeeding are mistakes made by many in the past which typically results in inadequate weight or obesity.

Not giving your harlequin the balanced diet it needs not only hinders it from doing all the wonderful, physical activities it likes and needs to do, it could also cause mental health deficiency which could lead to your naturally intelligent harlequin to become dull and lackluster. On the other hand, giving too much of something could also spell health issues for it. Many foods for human consumption are not advisable for harlequins and you have to know about these as well.

This chapter is geared to reveal to you what you need to know about the sort of foods your harlequin requires for a healthy mind and body as well as what it is allowed to eat and may like. Since your harlequin has a pretty accessible group of foods it can have and readily available commercially, you won't find it very difficult to provide for it daily. However, there are also quite a number of foods that you may not and cannot give your harlequins which you need to be aware of. Let's find out about all these in detail.

The Nutritional Needs of Rabbits

Apart from keeping its habitats, as cages, hutches and other furnishings and fitting in them, pristine, and disinfected, the provision of proper foods in diet of your rabbit will be very important to its health. Your rabbit is an innate grazer and a veggie eater who needs a high fiber diet.

The fiber in its food allows their gastrointestinal system to function gradually and consistently. If not given enough fiber in its diet your harlequin rabbit could get diarrhea, and that is not good news and could be deadly for the rabbit. Another illness which they could develop due to lack of fiber intake is gastro intestinal stasis wherein a rabbit ceases to eat, will not have bowel movements, or if it does, stool is runny and liquid instead of the usual dry and pellet-shaped stool. These conditions are silent and misleading and could cause the rabbit to die suddenly. So give your harlequins the correct amount of fiber rich foods.

Rabbit protein should measure 14-16% of the food pellets you purchase with 4% fat and a good 18% measure of fiber. Anything higher than an 18% protein content in baby rabbit diet is too high for them, so be careful to mind this. However, it is encouraged that a pregnant and nursing harlequin be given a slightly more protein in its diet and speaking of purchasing rabbit food is very wary of what sort of food you buy. Not all rabbit foods have the proper nutritional content which would meet the values needed by your rabbit. Make sure that you understand what food manufacturer labels mean and learn to decipher manufacturer jargon.

Do not forget the most basic of its nutritional need and that is fresh water all the time and lots of it. A fresh supply of clean drinking water is essential to any living being and this goes for your bunny as well.

Tips for Feeding Harlequin Rabbits

Always keep tabs of what you are feeding your rabbits. Be mindful that they are not underfed or over fed as either can tip the scales and cause the harlequin to become quite ill. Weigh your feed and measure the amounts being given.

If possible keep a journal of what is fed to them. This allows you to not second guess yourself should something go wrong. You can always refer back to your harlequin journal for information you may need regarding its health. Do not forget to give it hay as hay is low in fat, carbohydrate and relatively low protein content but high in fiber. Not only does it help its intestinal system function as it should, it also allows the rabbits to trim down their teeth as well.

Chapter Six: Breeding Your Harlequin Rabbit

Remember that you will need to have adequate space, housing and the proper equipment and furnishings if you intend to breed your harlequins. It is strongly advised that you network with recently successful breeders to gain tips, garner suggestions and best practices before you attempt to do this on your own. There are basic laws and ordinances you would also have to follow which your state or regional area of residence has, so be sure to find out by calling your local municipality officials who can channel you and your queries to the proper animal society authorized by your locale.

Mating Behavior of Rabbits

Most breeders will not breed their rabbits if they are below 5 months of age. But in fact rabbits are ready to breed into its 4 and a half month age. It is advisable to wait until the 5th or 6th month of the rabbit before it is bred out to another of the same sort. Never cross breed one rabbit sort with another rabbit kind.

Another reminder is to not mate a sickly rabbit to another. Make sure that the pairing are both healthy and of good nature. Check for signs of illness like runny stool, sores, discharge in any orifice (eyes, ears, genitals, vents). In addition, do not inbreed rabbits that are related or have genetic defects.

Rabbits can mate and get pregnant several times a year so be mindful that you do not mix in your rabbits together unless you are planning to raise a whole slew of young hoppers on top of the existing adult rabbits. You will also want to keep a journal of breeding events to keep tabs on the dates and have a clear idea of when to expect bunnies to start popping out.

When you decide that you are ready to breed the rabbits and when the rabbits are of appropriate age, you may bring the doe to the bucks cage and never the other way around as a buck in a doe's cage would just be the inquisitive visitor that it is an be more interested in inspecting and investigating its new surroundings and ignore the doe. It is a good idea to mate the buck with two does to ensure a good successful mating that would result in pregnancy.

Observe that they are getting along with each other because some females may not show interest. If this is the case, you will want to separate them but keep them in close proximity of each other in individual cages and try again the next day.

When the harlequins are ready for each other and agreeable to breed, the buck will mount the doe. This procedure is fast and quick. Once the buck is done, it would typically fall off from the doe and on its back. Separate them again and bring the doe back to its cage. To ensure a successful breeding process, you may repeat this again after 12 hours.

Once you are satisfied and are sure that the two rabbits have successfully mated remove the doe from the male harlequin's enclosure and return it to its cage.

Nesting Requirements

During the mating process you will have to set up the cage of the female to get it ready to nest and prep the area for gestation (the nesting period of a pregnant doe) as well as kindling (the birthing process of the rabbit). Let's have you focus on what you need and how to prepare for this period as a successful mating means a wait of about 31 days for the pregnant bunny to give birth.

When you are sure that the doe is pregnant and have confirmed this with a vet, you will want to place a nesting box in the doe's cage on the 28th day. Make sure that the pregnant harlequin's cage is lined with fresh bedding, preferably hay. She will most likely begin pulling fur from her belly to line her nest, so do not be alarmed by the seemingly strange act of her doing so. This is just matures way of ensuring that the babies she kindles will stay warm and snug when they arrive.

Make sure that the pregnant harlequin is making her nest inside the nesting box and not on the floor of the cage as this would mean that the babies born will not get enough heat and may expire. Baby bunnies not given the proper heating temperatures would least likely survive, so assist her with gentle care and move the nest into the nesting box.

Give her space and be very careful not to startle or frighten her as this could cause her stress. Minimize any sudden noises and keep the area where she is nesting free of chaos. Avoid handling or disturbing her and let her be.

Requirements of a Pregnant Harlequin Rabbit

As previously mentioned in the nutritional needs section, a pregnant harlequin will need more protein in her diet during this period, so be sure to consult with your animal physician about how to switch up the ratio and frequency of feeding a pregnant harlequin. Ask about any supplementary vitamins that the harlequin needs to be given and provide these if required.

Raising Baby Harlequin Rabbits

Newly kindled bunnies are usually hairless and are born blind, so do not be surprised when you see them. Make sure that the babies are birthed inside the nest and if this is not the case, then you should intervene and move them inside the nesting box. Keep in mind that the dam (mother) will not relocate her babies, so you will have to do so. As long as you do not disturb the mother, she will be fine with you handling her babies.

The harlequin dam would usually begin nursing the newborns on the 2nd day of their arrival, however, if she does not you may want to find them a foster dam that had recently given birth. Rabbits will foster another dams rabbit bunnies if the bunnies are within 4 days of each other; any older and it won't be allowed into another dams brood.

Keep the babies with their mother until about one and a half months after their birth, even though bunnies will start eating solid food at around 14 days of age. Some would even extend their stay with their mothers up to 6 weeks, but it will be up to you to separate them at this time and not allow them to be around their mother beyond their third month.

Chapter Seven: Grooming and Litter Training Your Harlequin Rabbit

You have learnt that the teeth of harlequin rabbits, unlike human teeth, do not stop growing and have been given the low down on what is required to keep those ever-growing teeth at bay to avoid mouth injuries to the rabbit. In this chapter we shall discuss the grooming needs of your harlequin to make sure that all bases are covered when it comes to the maintenance and care of your harlequin as well as how to litter train them.

Keeping Your Harlequin Rabbit Clean and Groomed

To help distribute essential skin oil evenly and to prevent any excessive shedding of fur, bruising its fur regularly will be a requirement to be done. You will need to check each of its sweat glands, especially when you notice a stench emanating from your rabbit. Its sweat glands can be found on either side of its reproductive organ.

You will have to make sure that there is no crusty build up in those areas. It could be tedious to pick these out by hand and some of you may get iffy about picking it up with bare hands. You can use a pair of thin gloves.

Should you spot ticks, fleas or mites on your rabbit are mindful of the removing agent your use as many of these flea products are harmful and poisonous to rabbits. Seek out the mildest product, preferably ones used on kitten, but again as precaution, you want to ask your vet about their recommended product and brand to use on the rabbit. To avoid ticks and fleas, limit your rabbit's exposure to animals that may carry the pests and raise your rabbit indoors. Avoid leaving them out in their hutches during months when fleas are more prevalent.

Last but not the least; your rabbit will need a routine clipping of its nails. Allowing their nails to grow too long could make it difficult for your rabbit to move. Overgrown and unkempt nails may snag on a wire, carpet, or the base of their enclosure and cause them injury.

When clipping your rabbit's nails, you want to make sure that it doesn't move around too much. The way to limit its movement is by swaddling it with a blanket, much like a burrito. Make sure that the blanket is not wrapped around it too tightly that it constricts but also not too loosely that it can get away. This procedure can be carried out with better ease when two people are present.

Once you have wrapped up your bunny and have it securely and comfortably situated on your lap you want to expose its paws one at time. If you notice too much squirming from your harlequin you may want to cover its eyes to get it to calm down.

Now, take your time trimming its nails and be mindful that you do not cut too deeply or you run the risk of cutting into the quick of its nails. This will cause profuse bleeding. In the event that this happens, you will need to stop the bleeding. Ask your vet what product you can use to do this. Rule of thumb when cutting its nail, don't cut too far into the nail.

Recommended Grooming Tools

You want invest on a study pair of rabbit nail clippers because you will be using this for a long time. Another thing you want to get is a good, soft brush to use for your routine brushing and grooming of the rabbit.

A blanket of its own as well as couple of towels for times when you need to wipe down you rabbit are other things you want to use exclusively for your rabbit and should you have more than one rabbit make sure that each of them get their own supplies and not borrow from each other.

Since you will hardly ever have to give you harlequin a bath, make sure that you at least have mild rabbit soap handy at all times. You will also want to have its own supply of cotton pads and cotton balls to use when cleaning out its ears and sweat glands.

Tips for Bathing and Grooming Harlequin Rabbits

It is not recommended to give harlequins a bath so ask your vet if you would need to if it is absolutely necessary and what you can do other than giving it a bath. Brushing its coat and giving it a wash with a damp cloth on areas where it has picked up dirt would be sufficient if absolutely needed, such as if it gets food stuck on itself.

Very rarely would rabbits need a bath, because like cats, they often groom themselves on their own. However, when they do need one remember not to soak the rabbit in water or give them a full bath. Zero in on grimy areas instead and be sure that the water is lukewarm so as not to scald or shock the rabbit with water too hot or too cold.

A hose would come in very handy to wash its backside or vent area. Keep in mind to ask your vet for recommendations on soaps and shampoo that are safe for your rabbit because most dog and cat cleaning products are toxic to them. Products for kittens are suitable for them because these are mild, but you should still get that vet recommended brand.

Other Grooming Reminders

Be mindful that you religiously brush your harlequin as this time with them not only give both of time to cuddle up with you and be sociable and be trained, it also allows you the time to inspect your bunny and get a closer look for any signs of fleas, scars, open sores, discharge or bad odor.

Litter Training Your Rabbit

We will be honest with you; potty training your rabbit will not be as easy as litter training a cat, a little more challenging than potty training a dog, but given the proper measure of patience, time and resources - in this case, litter boxes and more than a few of these, you and your rabbits will soon reap success.

Persevere during this time and steady yourself, most especially if you have more than a couple of rabbits living with you. Treats will help along with your attitude of patient teaching. When the rabbit is out of its cage, make sure that you have more than a few litter boxes strategically placed around the house where it can "go" and doo-the-deed.

It may take a while before your rabbits get it but if the harlequin is clever enough to recognize its name being called, trust that with your positive, encouraging attitude that it will all be well worth the time you spend teaching it to go to the "bathroom".

Handling and Taming Your Rabbit

Your harlequin is a clever animal and an accommodating one at that. Treat it with respect and it will grow up with this trait of reverence to you as well. They are perfect pets for young children, but with caution and care, you will have to supervise these visits and explain to younger children how to handle and play gently with your new harlequins. Never tug or pull on its ears or limbs. Do not yank its fur nor poke it.

You want your rabbits to associate you with gentleness and goodness. You don't want it traumatized by roughhousing or punishment. You will be at a better advantage if you raise your rabbit from the time it weans from its mother. But if acquiring a more mature rabbit, the situation could be a lot different.

First off, feeding time is usually a good time to work on training and taming your rabbit because you will want to use treats to reward good behavior. When the rabbit is initially introduced to your home, it may appear apprehensive and suspicious. Look out for body language and if you notice it to be uptight and wound up, leave training for another day. Visit with it frequently and talk to it in low tones until it gets used to your presence.

When it does get used to you, try coaxing it to come close to you from within its confines. Lay low beside its cage and do not loom over it so your rabbit doesn't mistake you for a predator. When it does come to you, stroke it gently from between the cage bars and give it time to get to know your scent. You can go on to the next step once it approaches you with confidence from within its cage.

You want to allow it sometime outside of its cage inside of a room which you have rabbit-proofed. Open the cage door and have it come out on its own. Like cats, rabbits will try to avoid you if you charge after it as a way of getting close to it. Instead let it come to you, and when it does, give it a pellet or fruit treat.

Make time for your rabbit and allow it to get used to your presence, your voice and your scent. Do this every day and be consistent about your tone of voice, the handing of treats and tender pats. Speaking of patting, pat and stroke it from behind its neck down to its back. Never hover your hand on top of its head or in front of its face lest it considers the gesture a threat and respond with a bite.

When picking up a rabbit, remember to do it sparingly and only when needed, such as when you need to clean its cage or groom it; you can do this by picking it up from the back of its neck, much like how a cat would carry its kitten, with your other hand stabilizing it under its belly.

Keep in mind that rabbits will get the urge to mate a few times a year (we will discuss this further in the book) and during this period, rabbits may seem a little more aggressive and try to nip you. You can avoid this by getting it either neutered or spayed. This operation will take a typically aggressive rabbit but if this is what you decide to do, give it about a month before you see the more gentle effects of the procedure.

Take note of actions that make it happy. Like a cat, harlequin rabbits may purr with delight, so aside from body language, watch out for this other cue that signals its ease. They are docile, friendly, intellectual and playful. These innate traits will only be magnified to magnificent heights if you are mindful enough to remember that they are to be treated with loving care.

Chapter Eight: Showing Your Harlequin Rabbits

If you want to show off your amazing and good – looking rabbit, why not try signing them up for showing competitions? You just need to follow and learn about the specific guidelines and standards of Harlequin rabbits as suggested by ARBA so that you can make sure that your pet is ready for a show. Read on to find out what these specifications are because this could help Harlequin aficionados prepare for a spectacular display.

Harlequin Rabbit Breed Standards

Both the color along with the harlequin's distinct markings makes up 75 of 100 points according to the Standard, which leaves fur at only 15 point, followed by its condition at only 5, rounding up with general type at only 10.

The perfect design of a harlequin pattern has 5-7 bands or bars of interchanging colors on its body. The colors on its face have to be divided evenly down the center. The harlequin's ears and feet must likewise interchange its colors. The ideal motif is almost impossible to achieve. The two kinds of harlequins are the Japanese harlequins and the magpie harlequins who display colors of blue, lilac, chocolate and black.

The ideal weight of a senior buck of six months or older is 7 1/2 lbs. The ideal weight of a senior doe 6 months and over is 8 lbs.

Junior bucks under the age of 6mths should not weigh over 7 1/2 lbs. and must have a minimum weight of 3 3/4 lbs. A junior doe under the age of 6 months should have a minimum weight of 3 3/4 lbs. and should not weigh over 8lbs.

The general type makes up 10 points. The cranium, ears and physique has to be ample and displayed with grace.

The ears should stick out like a "V". The span of the back legs must be a tad wider when compared to the span of the shoulders of the harlequin. The harlequin's top line must start from the nape slowly rising to utmost tip above the back legs sloping to the tail. They should also have medium-size bones. Faults are found for a huge or block shaped cranium; dewlap in excess, a stubby physique; ears too short.

The fur of the harlequin makes up a total of 10 points and has to be displayed as fly back fur sort and is to conform to the commercial normal fur standard of the ARBA.

The colors of the harlequin makes up a total of 15 points with the breakdown of point distribution as follows; colors are to be lush and vivid. One color should not over power the other. The fawn color in the Japanese harlequin is to be a muted orange and appears in line with muted color markings of lilac and blue.

The color clarity makes up 10 points and should be well seen and easily identified. Interchanging colors must not blend in and should be clear. Faults are found if there is too much matting, spotting or bridling as well as a unacceptable distribution of color. Disqualification is meted when there are white patches on the Japanese harlequin, such as beneath the jowls, around its eyes or tail and belly.

A total of 60 points make up the score for markings with the breakdown of point distribution as follows; the design on the harlequins back arch may be barred or banded or a combination of bars and bands. The lines are to be visibly clear, interchanging orange and black. The ultimate physical markings should be at least 5-7 interchanges of bars or bands displayed on either profile starting at the chest area of the harlequin.

An even division is black to 1/2 chest and forequarter beneath the 1/2 orange face. The orange 1/2 of the chest and beneath the forequarter 1/2 orange face. The 1/2 part of the orange chest and the beneath the hind leg beneath the black 1/2 face, showing a face framed in interchanging colors. Faults are found for too much bridling in the pattern of the physical color; as well as unsatisfactory harmony of colors on the sides of the harlequin stemming from a side which is unmarked by either band or bar. Disqualification is meted when the marking looks like a saddle or a Dutch belt.

The points given for head and ears are 20. The cranium of the harlequin is to be equally split with one side showing orange and the other black with 5 points given to each side of the cranium. The colors of the ears have to be vivid and distinct from top to bottom with one black the other orange. The orange side of the face has to be topped by a black ear and vice versa with 5 pts. given for each ear. Faults are found for abrupt and unsubstantial division, for ears displaying similar colors or for a cranium which does not interchange colors with the colors of its ears. Disqualification is meted when there is no clear divisible partition running down the mid-section of the harlequin's face.

Feet and legs are given 20 pts. If one foreleg is black and the other leg is orange in color and these colors are to be perfectly alternated with its hindquarters. The Japanese harlequins toenails may be mixed matched with light and dark hues or be light or dark. The toenails of the Magpie may be mixed matched or could be light or dark. Disqualification is called for a Japanese harlequin with white toenails. A total of 5 points is given for the harlequin's condition.

Preparing Your Rabbit for Show

You should have been in preparation mode months before a showing and would have also prepared your rabbit for display. Do this by giving you rabbit optimum nourishment. Grooming on a regular basis allows your harlequin to adjust its temperament in time for when it is showed to judges and it will help in keeping its fur lustrous and silky smooth.

Grooming and handling will create a trusting relationship between you and your harlequin equating to a stress-free rabbit, prepared to be displayed in front of other people. You will be at an advantage of knowing your harlequin's habits and body language. Do not neglect to trim the nails of your rabbit before the show.

Keep in mind that some shows compel you to register way in advance and there may be a fee to pay. Make certain that these are all taken care of so as to be allowed to join. Late entries may deem you to wait for another show to occur.

Make arrangements and get ready to gather all your rabbits grooming kit, toys and accessories for the trip. Taking your rabbit on semi-frequent trip will allow it to get used to being in a car and on the road. Do not forget its food and water supply and make sure that temperature in the automobile is conducive for your harlequin as you travel to the show site. Be punctual and get there way ahead of time to reduce the tension, rushing and stress.

Chapter Nine: Keeping Your Harlequin Rabbit Healthy

So you've learnt what you need to look out for when selecting a healthy rabbit to bring home with you. You've been let in on what to look out for when looking for a reputable rabbit breeder. You've studied up on what would be suitable cages, hutches and enclosures to use as well as materials these should be made out of.

You've also come to know what diet it needs to thrive well physically and mentally. Vaccinations it would need and the importance of preventing illnesses has been discussed as well. You've been advised on how to outfit not only its cage and hutch but also how to rabbit proof your home safely.

This time you want to zero in on what you need to do to keep your harlequin healthy. As you read on, you will find out about what it would take for you maintain its good health in order for it to lead a happy life with you.

Common Health Problems Affecting Harlequin Rabbits

Cage maintenance cannot be stressed enough when the discussion of pet health and wellness is on the table. As humans are susceptible and more prone to sickness in unsanitary conditions, more so are pets likelier to contract and be infected with disease and malaise when left to fester in germ-ridden environments.

Flystrike is a very common harlequin problem when a rabbit is not properly and correctly groomed. It is most prevalent around its rear area. Flystrike is an utterly gross skin condition when flies get attracted to the backside region of a rabbit, then burrows and lays eggs under the rabbit's skin!

This would cause maggots to infest beneath the skin of the rabbit which would lead to open sores that get infected if not treated immediately. Avoid this situation at all costs and make sure that you groom your rabbit regularly, checking for soiled patches of fur in that bottom region of your harlequin.

Overfeeding can lead to obesity and cause your harlequin to lead a stagnant, sedentary lifestlye. Watch your harlequin's diet and give it only the proper ratio of food as well as the acceptable kind for its sort. A bad diet can lead to diarrhea and can also be an issue when a rabbit is overfed with the sort of food it shouldn't have.

Have a decent amount of hay always available for your harlequin and a lot of greens and roughage like kale, and greens high in fiber because these would help your rabbit naturally wear down its teeth. Unlike us, the teeth of the harlequin never stops growing and if this is left unchecked and unmaintained could result in mouth injuries which would lead to difficulty chewing and eating properly. Symptoms of overgrown teeth and its effects would include a loss of appetite, a runny nose, eye discharge and lethargy.

Preventing Illness

Having your rabbits go in for a regular annual checkup gives you an advantage of knowing whether or not there is anything amiss with your rabbit's health. Keeping your harlequin from getting ill will is much easier if you know what to do from the onset to prevent them. First rule of thumb is to maintain cage sanitation at all times to avert any infestations of any sort.

Remember that unkempt and soiled cages and hutches are breeding grounds for virus, bacteria and even insects which spread disease and infection. So make it a habit of cleaning out your harlequin's cage everyday of soiled bedding, and schedule in weekly and monthly sanitation tasks.

Make sure that you replace any and all items that are used up and worn out, like gnawing twigs, beat up rolls of cardboard tubes, and soiled bedding. Make sure that uneaten food is cleared out of its dish daily and no moisture is trapped which become a nesting haven for bacteria and such.

Give your rabbit the proper amount of fiber in its diet as we discussed earlier or run the awful risk of sudden rabbit death caused by GI stasis. Other causes for gastrointestinal stasis is dehydration, it could also be related and caused by another illness unbeknownst to you like an infection, urinary tract disorders, gas, dental problems, or intestinal blockage. If not caught early the slowdown and complete halt of usual intestinal movement, this results to a painful sudden, death. Should your rabbit not eat or pass stool in a span of 12 hours, rush it to the vet right away!

Vaccinations for Your Harlequin

As an extra measure of safety geared toward the good health of your harlequin, remember to take your rabbits to the vet for a thorough once over before heading back home. Of course, your breeder - as long as you deal with one who is honest and upfront about their methods and procedures carried out for the rabbit before your purchase, would have done all the necessary initial steps to ensure a healthy rabbit is being handed over to you. However, all responsible pet owners has to get their own assurances and would want to introduce their new pet to their vet immediately after purchase and not simply hike on over to the medical expert when something goes array.

You would have ideally discussed vaccination and vaccination schedules for your harlequin with your vet and would have made this particular appointment to get your harlequin inoculated for initial shots it may need to protect it against and prevent Rabbit Hemorrhagic Disease. This is a viral medical condition causing great suffrage to rabbits accompanied by internal bleeding, horribly high fever and causes liver disease if left unchecked. RVHD is usually contracted by more mature rabbits with juvenile ones spared. It is commonly seen in feral rabbits in Britain and is almost always fatal. The HVRD is spread through contact from an infected rabbit to a healthy one. The virus thrives in unsanitary conditions, is carried through clothing, by insects and passed or transmitted through contact. Only vaccination can prevent this virus from affecting your rabbit as there is no cure once the rabbit is infected.

Myxomatosis is another deadly condition that is contracted from infected insect carriers like mites, mosquitoes and fleas. Symptoms of this virus include swelling and puffiness around the eyes, ears and face which typically causes blindness. The virus would eventually spread to the rabbit's genitals and anal area. Other symptoms include high grade fever, loss of appetite for food and difficulty in taking in water. There are some occasions when myxomatosis is extended accompanied by lumps. Death is almost certain if not given the proper inoculation at the onset of the harlequin's life. If your rabbit contracts this virus there is no treatment available except when caught early and rabbit is given intensive medical attention. If not detected early the best and worst option you are given is euthanasia.

Is Your Rabbit Ill?

Learning what to do and applying what you learn to give the rabbit a good chance for a healthy life is the start of a great friendship. However, realistically speaking, there will be off chances that your rabbits could get sick. When and if this does happen, you want to immediately quarantine the sick rabbit to prevent others from catching sickness, and bring it to a vet immediately.

There are telltale signs that you will be able to notice right off the bat if you take the time to get to know each of your rabbits individually on a personal level. Like every individual, there are telling signs of illness that would raise a red flag when you recognize it. It is important that you know how to identify these to avoid an ill rabbit from getting any sicker than it is.

This is an opportune time to remind you that the services of an experienced vet is vital to you and your rabbits, so have one on your list of emergency number, just in case. At this point we want to let you in on how to look out for signs of possible illnesses.

Should you notice your usually active harlequin suddenly refuse to move and lose back leg mobility, if it avoids any sort of movement or hopping, bring it to the vet. Should you notice any nasal or eye discharge, should it be drooling or show wet around its mouth, bring it to the doctor.

If the usually hardy eater refuses to accept food or drink water, that is a red flag that needs to be checked out by a medical expert. Any swelling, loss of fur or redness of skin deems a visit to the animal doctor as soon as possible. Not doing its "business" or signs of diarrhea, or dark urine is another red flag. And last but not the least, if your harlequin is running a fever of over 105 degrees, bring it to the vet.

How to Find the Ideal Rabbit Vet

Ask for referral from your friends who are also rabbit keepers. Chances are they know vets who are rabbit experts. You can also look at various rabbit organizations for a list of recommended rabbit vets. These vets applied to be on the recommended list and were approved by these organizations which mean that they somehow pass the standards. Another thing you can do is to check other sources online to find your preferred vet or someone who is really knowledgeable. You can always go to their clinic and interview them to see if you like them. You have to make sure that the rabbit vet you prefer are aware of the importance of hospitalizing rabbits.

A good rabbit vet knows that just in case your rabbit will need hospitalization, it should be placed in a separate kennel area away from other animals because the sounds of dogs, cats or other animals can be very stressful for rabbits since they are prey animals and may hinder recovery. This is an important thing to consider in finding your ideal rabbit vet.

Chapter Ten: Perks of Being a Rabbit Keeper

One of the perks of being a rabbit breeder or keeper is that you can earn an additional income out of them through selling the rabbits themselves, their meat or even their manure! In this chapter, you'll learn a thing or two on how to make this fun hobby profitable and also beneficial to other potential keepers or breeders like you.

Sell Your Rabbit's Manure

Did you know that a single rabbit can produce several yards of manure every year? In fact, according to some sources a doe and her offspring can even produce more than 1 ton of manure per year which makes it perfect for those of you who want to make money out of manure! It is always nice to be able to make additional revenue off of your rabbit project even if you are only into rabbit raising for a hobby. There are two ways you can do to increase your revenues when it comes to raising rabbits. You can sell their manure or sell it as fertilizers and/or grow your own worms under rabbit hutches, then sell it as fish bait.

Rabbit manure contains calcium and sulphur that are important ingredients in creating a healthy fertilizer. It also improves the soil's structure by adding organic matter and some beneficial micronutrients.

The manure of your Harlequin rabbit or any other rabbit breeds is considered a cold manure. Cold manures can be directly applied in garden soil without the need for composting, and it will also not burn plants because the nitrogen in cold manures are not readily available. For some rabbit farmers though, they choose to compost their rabbit's manure first to avoid the transfer of pathogenic diseases to crops or vegetables.

You can sell your rabbit manure as plant fertilizer because rabbit manure is by far one of the most valuable types of fertilizer in the world! The reason for this is because rabbit food is high in protein and quality which results in the natural development of a very high quality rabbit manure. Rabbit fertilizer is valuable to people who plant gardens and it even works great if you apply it to orchards according to most rabbit enthusiasts.

The bottom line is that rabbit manure can be a great source of nutrients and organic matter for your garden; it can save you money if you're already breeding more than one or two rabbits and it can potentially be another source of income if you choose to sell it to other farmers that needs fertilized soil.

Additional Income Stream

If you are raising one of the more fancy breeds of rabbits you should put more emphasis on markings and fur. These rabbits that exhibit these traits are bound to be your best producers due to the fact that they tend to carry the most desirable dominant genes. A little small rabbit might make a nice pet for someone but if you want to produce a quality breeding stock then make sure that they meet these physical requirements/qualities because usually large healthy parents tend to produce healthy offspring. Regardless of whether you are breeding for meat, as household pets, show animals or for wool, it is important to keep nice big healthy rabbits. Ideally, you want to breed rabbit stock that has broad shoulders, a good loin, and good hindquarters.

When you are running any type of business it is important to develop a good reputation amongst customers and potential buyers. So make sure that you offer reasonable prices and help your customers get started with their rabbit adventure by answering questions that your customers ask you to the best of your ability.

You should also give your customers an honest evaluation of the rabbits that you are selling. It's also ideal to attend any local rabbit meetings or clinics around your area so you can meet other rabbit enthusiasts and gain more knowledge and have a great time raising these cute bunnies.

Marketing Your Rabbitry

- Make sure to place your phone number or email address on your business card/website/social media page/flyers/ online ads etc. If you have a website URL, be sure to put that on the promotional material too. However, make certain that buyers have an alternate way to contact you other than through the internet.

- It is a good idea to distribute your home phone number instead of your cell number on your promotional material/s or website. Ideally if you have a fulltime rabbit business you will have your own business phone number but if you don't, then just put your home phone number instead or perhaps a public cellphone number.

- Email is another good way to communicate with potential customers online. In fact, most breeder directories including rabbitbreeders.us list the email addresses of rabbit breeders on the listing pages.

- Make sure to make a special email address for your rabbitry business. You can go to gmail.com and create a free email account. If you ever change email addresses, instead of trying to update your breeder listings and promotional material then you can just forward the messages to your new email address for less hassle.

Glossary of Rabbit Terms

Agouti – A type of coloring in which the hair shaft has three or more bands of color with a definite break between.

Albino – A pink-eyed, white-furred rabbit.

ARBA – The American Rabbit Breeders Association; an organization which promotes rabbits in the United States.

Awn – The strong, straight guard hairs protruding above the undercoat in angora breeds.

Bangs – Longer fur appearing at the front base of the ears and on top of the head in some woolen breeds.

Base Color – The color of the fur next to the skin.

Bell Ears – Ears that have large tips with distinct fall.

Belt – The line where the colored portion of the coat meets the white portion, just behind the shoulders.

Blaze – A white marking found on the head of the Dutch rabbit; the shape is wedge-like.

Bonding – A term used to describe two rabbits that have paired up together.

BRC – The British Rabbit Council, formed from the British Rabbit Society and the National Rabbit Council of Great Britain in 1934.

Broken Coat – Guard hairs that are missing or broken in places, exposing the undercoat.

Buck – An intact male rabbit.

Buff – A rich, golden-orange color.

Caecotroph – Pellets of semi-digested food eaten from the anus for nutrition reasons.

Chinning – Rubbing the chin on objects of people to spread scent from glands under the chin.

Cobby – A term meaning stout or stocky in body; short legs.

Condition – The overall physical state of a rabbit in terms of its fur, health, cleanliness, and grooming.

Crossbreeding – Mating two different breeds.

Cull – The process of selecting the best rabbits from a litter and selling or slaughtering the rest.

Dam – A female rabbit that has produced offspring.

Doe – An unaltered female rabbit.

Flat Coat – Fur lying too close to the body, lacking spring and body as noted by touch.

Fryer – A young meat rabbit no more than 10 weeks of age and weighing less than 5 pounds.

Gestation – The period of time between breeding and birthing (or kindling).

Guard Hair – The long, coarser hairs in a rabbit's coat which protect the undercoat.

Herd – A group of rabbits.

Inbreeding – Breeding of closely related stock.

Junior – A class of rabbits referring to those under 6 months of age.

Kindling – The process of giving birth to baby rabbits (kits).

Kindling Box – A box provided for a pregnant rabbit so she can make a nest and give birth.

Kit – A baby rabbit.

Line Breeding – A breeding program in which rabbits that are descended from the same animal are bred.

Litter – A group of young rabbits born to one doe at the same time.

Loose Coat – Fur conditions in the undercoat, often coupled with smooth hair resulting in not so good texture.

Malocclusion – A misalignment of the rabbit's teeth.

Molt – The process of shedding or changing the fur, happens twice each year.

Nest Box – A box provided for a pregnant rabbit so she can make a nest and give birth.

Nursing – The process of kits suckling milk from the dam's teats; usually occurs twice a day.

Peanut – A rabbit with two dwarf genes; usually fatal.

Pelage – The fur coat or covering in a rabbit.

Pellets – May refer either to the rabbit's poop or its food.

Quick – The pink part of the nails/claws that contains the blood vessels and nerves.

Racy – Referring to a slim, slender body and legs.

Saddle – The rounded portion of the back between the rabbit's shoulder and loin.

Self-Colored – A fur pattern where the hair colors are the same all over the body.

Sire – A male rabbit that has produced offspring.

Thumping – The practice of banging or stomping the hind legs on the ground to make a loud, thudding noise.

Ticking - A wavy distribution of longer guard hairs throughout the rabbit's coat.

Weaning – The process in which baby rabbits become independent of their dam, transitioning to solid food.

Wool – A term used to describe the fur of Angora rabbits

Index

Photo Credits

References

Basic Information - TheNatureTrail.com

http://www.thenaturetrail.com/rabbit-care/basic-information/

Guidance: Caring for rabbits – UK Government

https://www.gov.uk/government/publications/rabbits-on-farm-welfare/caring-for-rabbits

Breeding Harlequin Rabbits - GeoCities.ws

http://www.geocities.ws/checkerboardrabbits/

Grooming a Rabbit - HopperHome.com

http://www.hopperhome.com/grooming_a_rabbit.htm

Harlequin - Pets4Homes.co.uk

https://www.pets4homes.co.uk/breeds/rabbits/harlequin/

Harlequin Rabbit - RoysFarm.com

http://www.roysfarm.com/harlequin-rabbit/

Harlequin Rabbit - PetGuide.com

http://www.petguide.com/breeds/rabbit/harlequin-rabbit/

How to Care for Harlequin Rabbits - WikiHow.com

http://www.wikihow.com/Care-for-Harlequin-Rabbits

Rabbit Sale Laws in the U.S. - WabbitWiki.com

http://wabbitwiki.com/wiki/Rabbit_sale_laws_in_the_US

Rabbit Vaccinations - Rspca.org.uk

https://www.rspca.org.uk/adviceandwelfare/pets/rabbits/health/vaccinations

Selecting a Healthy Rabbit - Petwebsite.co.uk

http://www.petwebsite.co.uk/rabbits/buying-a-rabbit/selecting-a-healthy-rabbit

Standard of the Harlequin Rabbit Breed - RabbitTalk.com

http://rabbittalk.com/harlequin-standards-t9495.html

The Bunny - From Conception to Weaning – Debmark.com

http://www.debmark.com/rabbits/bunnies.htm

Types of Rabbits - JustRabbits.com

http://www.justrabbits.com/types-of-rabbits.html

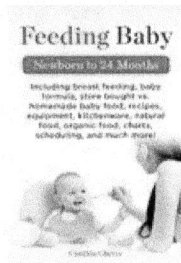

Feeding Baby
Cynthia Cherry
978-1941070000

Axolotl
Lolly Brown
978-0989658430

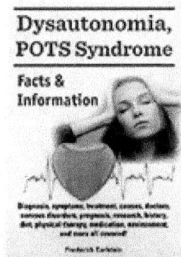

Dysautonomia, POTS
Syndrome
Frederick Earlstein
978-0989658485

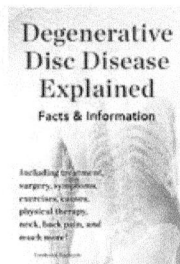

Degenerative Disc
Disease Explained
Frederick Earlstein
978-0989658485

Sinusitis, Hay Fever,
Allergic Rhinitis Explained
Frederick Earlstein
978-1941070024

Wicca
Riley Star
978-1941070130

Zombie Apocalypse
Rex Cutty
978-1941070154

Capybara
Lolly Brown
978-1941070062

Eels As Pets
Lolly Brown
978-1941070167

Scabies and Lice Explained
Frederick Earlstein
978-1941070017

Saltwater Fish As Pets
Lolly Brown
978-0989658461

Torticollis Explained
Frederick Earlstein
978-1941070055

Kennel Cough
Lolly Brown
978-0989658409

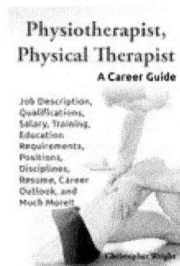

Physiotherapist, Physical
Therapist
Christopher Wright
978-0989658492

Rats, Mice, and Dormice
As Pets
Lolly Brown
978-1941070079

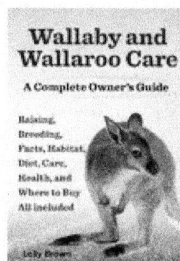

Wallaby and Wallaroo Care
Lolly Brown
978-1941070031

Bodybuilding Supplements
Explained
Jon Shelton
978-1941070239

Demonology
Riley Star
978-19401070314

Pigeon Racing
Lolly Brown
978-1941070307

Dwarf Hamster
Lolly Brown
978-1941070390

Cryptozoology
Rex Cutty
978-1941070406

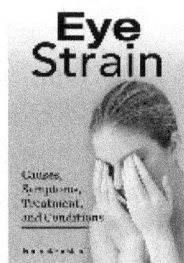

Eye Strain
Frederick Earlstein
978-1941070369

Inez The Miniature Elephant
Asher Ray
978-1941070353

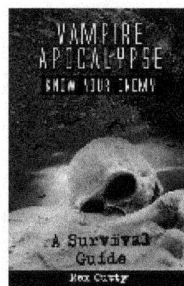

Vampire Apocalypse
Rex Cutty
978-1941070321

www.ingramcontent.com/pod-product-compliance
Lightning Source LLC
LaVergne TN
LVHW051648080426
835511LV00016B/2565